History's Greatest Artists: The Life and Legacy of Pablo Picasso

By Charles River Editors

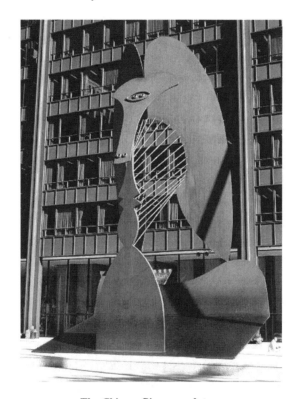

The *Chicago Picasso* sculpture

About Charles River Editors

Charles River Editors was founded by Harvard and MIT alumni to provide superior editing and original writing services, with the expertise to create digital content for publishers across a vast range of subject matter. In addition to providing original digital content for third party publishers, Charles River Editors republishes civilization's greatest literary works, bringing them to a new generation via ebooks.

Introduction

Pablo Picasso (1881-1973)

"Everyone wants to understand painting. Why don't they try to understand the song of the birds? Why do they love a night, a flower, everything which surrounds man, without attempting to understand them? Whereas where painting is concerned, they want to understand. Let them understand above all that the artist works from necessity; that he, too, is a minute element of the world to whom one should ascribe no more importance than so many things in nature which charm us but which we do not explain to ourselves. Those who attempt to explain a picture are on the wrong track most of the time." – Pablo Picasso, 1934

In their biography of Pablo Picasso, Hans Ludwig and Chris Jaffe note that "for him, art was always adventure: 'To find is the thing.'" Indeed, there is perhaps no artist who produced more art than Picasso, whose enormous oeuvre (which spanned most of his 91-year life) contained a countless number of paintings and drawings. Picasso also worked in other mediums as well, notably sculpture and lithography, and his constant experimentation with form makes him a useful case study through which to chart the growth of Modernism as an artistic movement and many of the artistic trends that would dominate the 20th century.

At the same time, one of the challenges involved in examining Picasso's body of work is the sheer breadth of it all. In addition to the many different mediums involved, Picasso's works within each medium also vastly differed. For example, placing the paintings of Picasso's Blue Period (1901-1904) against his analytic cubist compositions reveals little similarities, and in many ways, he also anticipated artistic movements such as Abstract Expressionism and Neo-Expressionism. And though he is most famous for his contributions to the Cubist genre, there is a wide disparity between his early analytic cubist works and the later synthetic cubist style.

Picasso is one of the world's most famous artists, which adds to the challenge of examining his career, but it's necessary to examine his entire career because of the way art was intertwined with his life. Even from an early age, it was clear that he subordinated any external concerns relating to his life in the interest of making art, which may have been the cause of the spirit of melancholy that can be found in his artwork. At the same time, the somber tone of some of his work can be directly contrasted against his playful formal experimentation.

History's Greatest Artists: The Life and Legacy of Pablo Picasso examines Picasso's life and career, while analyzing his painting style, artistic themes, and his legacy. Along with pictures of some of his most famous work, a bibliography, and a Table of Contents, you will learn about one of history's greatest painters like you never have before, in no time at all.

Chapter 1: Picasso's Early Years

"It is not what the artist does that counts. But what he is. Cézanne would never have interested me if he had lived and thought like Jacques-Émile Blanche, even if the apple he had painted had been ten times more beautiful. What interests us is the anxiety of Cézanne, the teaching of Cézanne, the anguish of Van Gogh, in short the inner drama of the man. The rest is false." – Pablo Picasso

Pablo Picasso was born on October 25, 1881 in Malaga, located on the southern coast of Spain in the province of Andalusia. The seaside location is of particular relevance when discussing Picasso's career, since it was located in close proximity to Africa, whose cultural heritage would fascinate Picasso as he grew older. Picasso was raised as a Catholic, and like many Catholic Spaniards, his full name was enormous: Pablo Diego Jose Francisco de Paula Juan Nepomuceno Maria de los Remedios Cipriano de la Santisima Trinidad Ruiz y Picasso. His father, Jose Ruiz Picasso, was a painter who would later become an art teacher, and he was a full 16 years older than his wife and already 41 years old at the time of Pablo's birth. Pablo was the eldest child, and he would eventually have three other siblings, all sisters. In the Spanish tradition, the family was large and close-knit, and Picasso cared deeply for his siblings.

The building where Picasso was born in Malaga

One area of disagreement among scholars concerns Picasso's family genealogy. As an artist and later art teacher, Picasso's father did not make a substantial income, and the family experienced significant poverty during stretches of his childhood as a result. However, others in Picasso's extended family were highly successful and affluent, suggesting that Picasso's pedigree contained some aspect of financial wealth. Ultimately, this meant that Pablo was likely exposed to elements of both poverty and affluence during his upbringing, and they would both characterize different periods of his adult life.

Although there is disagreement over the social standing of Picasso's ancestry, with some claiming that Picasso descended from the aristocracy, the more widely accepted belief, introduced by Ronald Penrose in his biography of the artist, holds that Picasso's oldest ancestors were gypsies, which would not have been uncommon in the south of Spain. Those who hold that Picasso's eldest ancestors were gypsies also contend that his genetic profile contains at least some semblance of Jewish ethnicity. If it is true that Picasso descended from gypsies, his later fascination with them would be perhaps more easily explained. In any case, Picasso held a deep empathy for peasants, which was particularly noticeable during the early periods of his career.

While there are still unresolved questions surrounding the nature of Picasso's family tree, what is clear is that understanding Picasso's upbringing is only possible through recognizing the strong extent to which Spanish culture is imbued with suffering and melancholia. There is an entire lineage of Spanish art that reflects themes of suffering, and Spain is often contrasted with France; where Spain represents suffering and exudes a sense of sadness, its northern neighbor embodies gaiety and happiness. The contrast in artistic styles also underscores the contrast between the two countries. Spanish artwork, dating back to El Greco and continuing through the works of Diego Velazquez and Francisco Goya, evinced a harshly realistic focus on human suffering.

In a similarly fateful vein, Picasso's childhood was filled with a series of tragedies that were commensurate with that of Spanish culture. Even his birth brought him into close contact with death; legend holds that Picasso nearly died while he was being born because the nurse believed he was stillborn. It was only after his uncle, Doctor Don Salvador, began smoking a cigar and the infant Pablo cried in reaction to the smoke that it became clear he was actually alive. Picasso was well aware of this story, and he remained cognizant of the fact that he had survived a close call with death at an early age, which helped him maintain a deep appreciation for living. While it is certainly true that elements of the story may be apocryphal, it is relevant to any analysis of his life and career since it reflects the strong role that death played in his life.

Picasso's early years were also filled with instances of tragedy. When he was 3 years old, the town of Malaga was hit with a severe earthquake that ravaged the city, and the mass destruction that resulted would remain with him for the rest of his life and inform his reaction to later instances of widespread demolition, environmental and otherwise. However, despite the earthquake, Picasso remained fond of Malaga, and his appreciation for seaside locales would also manifest itself later in his life. He enjoyed studying the local animals, particularly the doves and pigeons that populated the town square, and it's quite likely his predilection toward animals was influenced by the fact that animals were also the favored painting subject of his father.

Although his family enjoyed Malaga, Picasso's father was unable to make a sustainable income, and his career as an artist dwindled. It is important to remember that during the 19th century, there existed a hierarchy among the different painting genres, and paintings of animals received little prestige. Had Don Jose Ruiz specialized in portraiture, it is likely that he would have been more successful, but animal painting was simply not lucrative enough to provide for his growing family. Consequently, he accepted a position as art instructor for the School of Fine Arts in Corunna when Pablo was 10 years of age.

Corunna is similar to Malaga in that it is also a port town, but the climate in Corunna is vastly different because it's located on the northern coast of Spain. There is more cultural influence from France and northern Spanish cities like Barcelona and Madrid, the former of which would become one of Picasso's primary places of residence throughout his young adulthood. Still, the family lived a comfortable middle-class existence, even though Picasso's father held a deep-rooted disappointment in his own failed artistic career. Meanwhile, it was during this period in Corunna that Pablo himself began to paint at increasing levels, and his technique became refined beyond his years. Even before moving to the north of Spain, Picasso was recognized as an artistic prodigy, and his parents were fond of telling the story (the validity of which is unconfirmed) that the first words ever spoken by Picasso were "lapiz, lapis," which translates to "pencil, pencil." Whether or not the story is true, making art remained Picasso's dominant interest throughout his childhood.

At the age of 14, Picasso's family moved to Barcelona, though they still summered in Malaga, and by this point Pablo had refined his craft to such an extent that one legendary story explains the esteem with which Picasso's father viewed his son. When Pablo was 13, his father saw him painting and realized that his son had surpassed him in skill, and at that point Don Jose Ruiz permanently ended his own painting career. Although the story may be exaggerated or even false, it nevertheless conveys the talent possessed by Pablo even at an early age, despite having no formal training. It should be remembered that art books did not exist, and without visiting a museum, potential artists had no exposure to art. Although he had received instruction from his father, Pablo was to a large extent an autodidact, much like Vincent van Gogh.

En route to Barcelona, the Picasso family stopped in Madrid, home to the Prado museum. To this day, the Prado is the most decorated art museum in Spain, and it housed works from the most acclaimed painters of the Spanish canon, including Francisco Goya, El Greco, and Diego Velazquez. The artworks made a deep impression on Picasso, and he would remain impacted by their work over the entire course of his own career, evidenced by the fact that late in his career Picasso began making studies of the renowned Spanish painters' works. He was influenced by them on both formal and thematic levels; the somber, tragic tone of their works was of particular influence. Although he is known for exuding a sense of joie de vivre, Picasso always held a strong appreciation for the melancholic temperament that can be found in works such as *Los Caprichos* (The Vagaries), a series of 80 lithographs that Velazquez completed around the turn of the 19th century that conveyed psychological torment.

In addition to being the year in which Picasso moved to Barcelona, 1895 was a significant year in Picasso's life for more tragic reasons. En route from Corunna to Madrid, his seven year-old sister Conchita died of diphtheria. The death was prolonged, and understandably the teenaged Picasso had great difficulty watching his sister die in his presence. Not surprisingly, the difficulty he had in processing death would represent a particularly salient theme in the early stages of his artistic career.

On top of his sister's death, although Picasso came from a supportive, close-knit family, his upbringing included episodes of extreme tragedy that affected him his entire life. The constant reminder that he had nearly died immediately after being born, the poverty his family experienced as a young child in Malaga, and the death of his sister were all difficult events for the young Picasso to process. Faced with harsh realities at a young age, art could either represent an escape from the concerns of everyday life or a means through which to process difficult occurrences. The subject matter of his subsequent career clearly reflects how Picasso chose the latter approach. For Picasso, art was never an escape from reality but instead the exterior reflection of the way in which he interpreted the world around him. As Picasso would later put it, "Painting isn't an aesthetic operation; it's a form of magic designed as mediator between this strange hostile world and us."

The reputation that Picasso holds as a jovial and lively man among the general public today is vastly different than the personality he exhibited during his upbringing. When people discuss Picasso today, the artist is often framed as a playful, almost silly character who painted abstract compositions that make little sense. However, while it is true that Picasso was engaged in a constant dialogue with himself concerning artistic form, his early life was fraught with tragedy. Although there is some disagreement concerning certain details of his family history, it is also clear that certain traces of his family background would impact the artistic works he would later create.

Chapter 2: Art School

By the time his family had moved to Barcelona, Picasso exhibited a level of painting expertise that was far beyond his years. Although matriculation into the School of Fine Arts in Barcelona was not typically accomplished until adulthood (18 years or older), Picasso applied for admission in 1895 when he was still just 14 years old. He completed the rigorous application process within one week and was admitted. However, like many autodidacts, Picasso was not receptive to formal instruction and skipped class more often than not. Shortly after enrolling, he quit altogether.

Despite quitting art school almost immediately after having enrolled, there is an extant work by Picasso that was completed in the style promoted in the School of Fine Arts at the time. Titled *First Communion*, Picasso completed the work over parts of 1895 and 1896, and at first glance, the work bears virtually no similarities to Picasso's later works. While it is true that there is little similarity with regard to the formal qualities of the composition, the astute viewer can nevertheless find thematic relevance relating to Picasso's personal life up to that point. In particular, the religious subject matter corresponded with Picasso's own Catholic upbringing, while the seriousness of the subject's faces evokes traces of the tragedy that had subsumed his early life. On a formal level, the striking juxtaposition of black and red recalls the saturated colors associated with the works of Spanish painters like Francisco Goya. Ultimately, however, *First Communion* holds little connection with Picasso's mature works.

First Communion

The reasons for Picasso's distaste for formal artistic training are multifaceted. At the end of the 19th century, art schools impressed upon students the importance of learning a style of painting that was highly regimented and owed its origins to classical Renaissance painting. Students painted from models that were assigned to them, and everyone was taught to paint in the same manner. Always individualistic, Picasso eschewed the dogmatic approach of the School of Fine Arts and instead skipped class to paint outside, focusing on the street life of Barcelona. He painted compulsively; capturing the world as it hit him became a part of his life that would remain with him until his death.

Picasso's predilection for painting outdoors during this period is particularly significant when placed in the context of late 19th century Western Europe. To this end, it is important to acknowledge the profound significance of the Impressionist movement that had begun decades earlier in Paris. In the 1860s, artists such as Eduoard Manet, Auguste Renoir, and Claude Monet began painting everyday images of Paris outdoors, eschewing models and instead painting spontaneously to fully capture the flow of urban life. Breaking from the drawing style popularized in Renaissance painting, the Impressionists adopted a painterly style characterized by pronounced brushwork, natural light gradations, and a vibrant color palette. They worked at a fast pace and captured the world rather than painting subjects that escaped from it, thereby establishing a clear break from classical painting that would impact Western art in the 20th century.

Although he was situated in Barcelona rather than Paris, it is not difficult to see Picasso's rejection of formal instruction as an implicit embrace of the Impressionist movement. While he did not harbor the resentment toward more traditional painters that the Impressionists held, he favored working outdoors and conveying the landscape of everyday life. Moreover, he shared the Impressionists' emphasis on formal experimentation and painting in a non-naturalistic manner. Over the course of his career, Picasso was never concerned with representing the world in the sense of presenting precisely how it looked but instead painted in a manner that used artistic form to convey his psychological perspective on his subject.

Although he never identified himself as such, the young Picasso also shared many similarities with the *flaneur*, the man who strolled the urban streets absorbing the visual stimuli around him. A character type popularized by Charles Baudelaire, the *flaneur* was an avatar for modernity, a man who approached the everyday city climate as a spectacle. By spending his days on the street painting, Picasso essentially occupied the role of *flaneur*; while his impressions of the environment around him were not always celebratory, he held a deep fascination with the world around him that was commensurate with that of Baudelaire's iconic character type.

Picasso lived in Barcelona until 1897, at which time he decided at the urging of his father to attempt a formal art school education once again. Instead of enrolling in the School of Fine Arts in Barcelona, however, he matriculated in the Royal Academy of San Fernando, one of the most prestigious art schools in Western Europe. Madrid also afforded Picasso closer proximity to the Prado Museum, which undoubtedly served as an alternate site for education in the eyes of the young artist. During his art classes, Picasso became enraptured by the Pre-Raphaelites, a school of British painters from the mid-19th century whose style reflected little of the formal experimentation that would characterize Picasso's own career but emphasized human emotion in a manner that closely resembled the subject matter of Picasso's early works.

While in Madrid, Picasso completed many paintings, one of which is still considered among his masterpieces. Titled *Science and Charity*, the work conveys a priest delivering the last rites to a dying mother while a nun holds her baby. The painting, completed in 1897, bears a resemblance to *First Communion*, as the priest's long forehead recalls that of the bishop in *First Communion*. The painting is also loaded with religious symbolism, as the nun holds the baby in a manner evocative of the Madonna and Child symbol; through incorporating this symbolic motif, Picasso implicitly alerts the viewer that the mother is morally pure and her death was not caused by sin. The emotionally-charged, historical subject matter reflects the works of the Pre-Raphaelites, in particular William Michael Rossetti and Thomas Woolner. At the same time, the painting also reflects a more contemporary approach, evidenced by the visible brushwork and painterly composition. It is clear that Picasso did not draw the entire composition prior to painting it, as many of the shapes (most notably, the window) are indistinct.

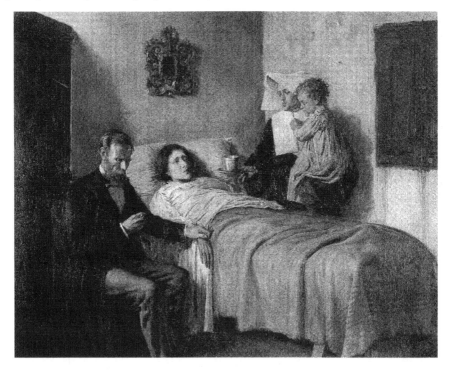

Paintings like *Science and Charity* reflect Picasso's growth as an artist, but the second attempt at receiving formal artistic training was no more successful than his first, and he did not complete his studies. Moreover, his health began to suffer, and in 1898 he contracted scarlet fever. The disease represented yet another instance in which Picasso was faced with the prospect of death, but his health eventually improved. He moved to Taragona, a city in northeastern Spain, but he did not stay long and was back in Barcelona by 1899.

At the turn of the century, Barcelona was the most exciting city in Spain for an aspiring young artist. Inspired by Paris, which at that time was an international artistic epicenter, Barcelona was a hub for artistic creativity, and the 18 year-old Picasso thrived in the environment. He particularly enjoyed the famous café Els Quatre Gats, a hip establishment that doubled as night club and café. At Els Quatre Gats, Picasso became acquainted with many avant-garde artists and thinkers, including famous architect Antonio Gaudi, draughtsman Ricard Opisso, musician Isaac Aldoniz, and founder Pere Romeau. The café also held galleries and was a pillar for artistic and philosophic discussion; fittingly, Els Quatre Gats was the site of Picasso's first exhibition in 1900.

Picasso's closest friend during this Barcelona period was Jaime Sabartes, a businessman who also maintained a hobby as a sculptor. Sabartes served as an early muse for Picasso, and it was with Sabartes that Picasso truly developed as a portrait artist, a genre that was held in the highest regard. Picasso's 1900 painting *Sabartes Seated* portrays his friend looking wan and melancholy, vaguely similar to the subjects of Goya's *Los Caprichos*. It is immediately apparent that *Sabartes Seated* represents a departure from the style evinced by *First Communion* or *Science and Charity*; his style is even sketchier, with a hurried appearance that looks as though it was completed quickly.

One of the ancillary advantages to living in Barcelona was its relative proximity to Paris, and Picasso visited Paris for the first time in 1900. Still recognized as the world's preeminent hub for art, Paris underwent a drastic artistic shift at the turn of the century. By the 1890s, the first wave of Impressionist painters had for the most part given way to a second generation of Impressionists, also known as the Post-Impressionists. This latter group included painters such as Paul Gauguin, Paul Cezanne, Georges Seurat, and Henri Matisse, the latter of whom would be inextricably positioned as Picasso's rival for the greater part of his career.

The main shift from the Impressionists to the Post-Impressionists was that the second generation experimented with form to an even greater degree, developing styles that were more singularly unusual. The first generation of Impressionists, like Auguste Renoir and Claude Monet, adhered to a formal methodology—visible brushstrokes, natural light, unsaturated colors—that was relatively similar. In contrast, the Post-Impressionists each had distinct styles, with the only commonality being that they were formally innovative. For example, where Matisse embraced bold, bright colors, Cezanne juxtaposed the geometric shapes of the objects he painted. Meanwhile, Gauguin, borrowing from the Japanese aesthetic, emphasized diagonal lines and flat compositions. Perhaps the most unusual of them all, Georges Suerat, developed the pointillist (also known as Neo-Impressionist) technique in which brushstrokes were replaced by visible tiny dots that gave the painting the appearance of a mosaic. As someone whose career would later be recognized as one of the most formally innovative in history, it is easy to see how Paris at the turn of the century made a strong impact on Picasso, particularly at a time in which he was still in the nascent stages of developing his technique.

One of the most notable aspects of Picasso's paintings, particularly his early ones, is the way in which he references other artists. While in Paris, Picasso painted works in which one can clearly observe the influence of reigning artists of the time. An example of one such painting is *Moulin de la Galette* (1900), a work that borrows from the styles of Toulouse-Lautrec, Vincent van Gogh, Eduoard Degas, and even Japanese art. The nightclub setting, reminiscent of the famous "Chat Noir" nightclub in Paris, resembles the setting of Toulouse-Lautrec's famous caricatures. Another Lautrec reference can be seen through the woman on the lower left of the painting, whose grin is simultaneously animated while also reflective of the mask-like emptiness evinced in the night-hall scenes of van Gogh. Meanwhile, the diagonal line of the white table reflects the compositions of both Degas and Japanese painters such as Hiroshige. Through paintings such as this one, the viewer gains an understanding for the way in which Picasso diligently studied the works of other renowned artists.

While in Paris, Picasso met Max Jacob, a good friend with whom he would live during his stay in Paris. In Jacob, Picasso effectively recreated the dynamic he had established with Jaime Sabartes in Barcelona, but unfortunately his time with Jacob was short lived because neither had any money, making their living situation all but unsustainable. At one point, in order to heat their living space, the pair relied on Picasso's paintings as firewood.

Faced with the need to move, Picasso would relocate to Madrid at the conclusion of 1900, but he would only live there for the first five months of 1901. Nevertheless, his tenure there was highly influential, as he and his friend Francesc d'Assis Soler founded the publication *Arte Joven*. Picasso served as illustrator for the magazine, which lasted for just five issues. Over his artistic career, Picasso would always be reticent to form artistic movements, which differed greatly from the utopian-minded artists of the Post-Impressionist movement like Vincent van Gogh and Paul Gauguin, who had held ambition for forming movements like artists' communes. Still, the youthfulness of the *Arte Joven* venture recalls the mentality of the Impressionists, whose eschewal of the artistic academy had proved influential in overturning the way in which the public viewed art.

Chapter 3: The Blue Period and Rose Period

"For a long time I limited myself to one colour — as a form of discipline." – Pablo Picasso, in reference to his "Blue" and "Rose" periods.

In the middle of 1901, Picasso moved back to Barcelona, where he would stay for the next three years. To a present-day observer, a three-year stay may not seem like a prolonged period, but it would constitute the lengthiest period in one location for Picasso since his time in Malaga, when he was young and still living with his family.

Ultimately, Picasso's time in Barcelona from 1901-1904 was filled with artistic developments and personal turmoil, and the relationship between artistic growth and personal tragedy would inform Picasso's oeuvre. Picasso's intense sadness was caused by the suicide of his close friend Carlos Casagemas, an event that was partly responsible for Picasso's decision to return to Barcelona. After the death of Casagemas, Picasso fell into an extreme depression, the most pronounced of his career, and he comprehensively overhauled his artistic style. Over the course of his career, Picasso made an effort to reflect his state of mind in the composition of each painting. For this reason, he once noted that "I paint objects as I think them, not as I see them." While this quotation is perhaps more germane to the deeply abstract works Picasso would make later in his career, his works from 1901 onward all hold extreme psychological resonance.

After Casagemas died, Picasso entered his Blue Period, which was so called to express his sorrow over the occurrence. The passing of his friend was yet another instance of death in a young life that had already been faced with death and near-death encounters. In certain respects, the Blue Period was not drastically different from Picasso's earliest works, but the major change he implemented was that the palette contained substantial amounts of blue, both in the foreground and background. The people in the Blue Period paintings appear to exist in a state of mourning commensurate with that of Picasso himself. Their bodies are gaunt and they do not look forward, as though they are too distraught to engage with the viewer.

Picasso's portrait of Sabartes

Perhaps Picasso's most famous work completed during the Blue Period was *La Vie*, which was also one of the earliest paintings of the period. In the painting, a naked woman embraces her spouse, who is clad only in a loincloth. Neither meets the viewer's gaze, and they are not affectionate with one another. To the right of the couple is a woman clad in a robe who holds a baby. In the background are two primitive drawings of a mother and child.

One of the most notable themes of the painting is the contrast between nudity and coldness. The preponderance of nudity would suggest an erotically-charged composition, yet the sterility of the color palette and the somber facial expressions exhibited by the characters represent the very antithesis of eroticism. Another thematic motif is the title; while *La Vie* invokes the reproductive cycle, the frowning expression exhibited by the woman on the right reflects a profound ambivalence toward raising children. It is also possible to read the painting's composition metaphorically, with the woman on the right representing the woman on the left at a later age, when she has become a mother. Such a reading suggests that the man has died by the time the woman reaches motherhood, which corresponds with the general despair of the Blue Period as a whole.

Picasso's other works in the Blue Period were equally somber. In another famous work from the period, *The Old Guitarist* (1903), Picasso conveys the melancholy act of a street performer in Barcelona.

In a sense, *The Old Guitarist* is even more severe than *La Vie*, since the subject is emaciated and appears in a near-death state. Certainly, the painting does not reflect the level of abstraction that would characterize Picasso's more mature works, yet Picasso takes artistic liberties that distance the work from simply capturing the world as he saw it. Each component of the painting, including the man's skin, his clothing, and the street surrounding him, is a different gradation of blue color, and only the guitar disrupts this relatively monochromatic palette. There is a balance between the hyper-realism of portraying an impoverished street musician and the expressive, non-naturalistic use of color deployed by Picasso.

Although *The Old Guitarist* is in some respects non-naturalistic, Picasso's technique nevertheless evinces a psychological realism that reflected the despondency he felt at the time. Describing his nonrepresentational use of color, Picasso once expressed the belief that "colors, like features, follow the changes of the emotions", a belief that corresponded with the prevailing ethos of the Post-Impressionists, as artists like van Gogh and Gauguin would use color to convey psychological states of mind. However, what is unusual about Picasso's use of color in his Blue Period is that he combines "psychological" color with a subject that is painted with an extreme, almost documentary realism. In the end, the painting reflects the central tension exhibited by the works from the Blue Period: the balance between representing interior and exterior reality. More than perhaps any other period of Picasso's career, the Blue Period is imbued with this thematic conflict.

The Blue Period is heavily emphasized in analyses of Picasso's oeuvre, likely because of the emotionally charged compositions and the heavy contrast between the works of the period and the ones Picasso would complete in the mature stages of his career, but it must be noted that the Blue Period lasted a relatively short time span of just three years. In 1904, Picasso moved to Paris and met a model named Fernande Olivier. Immediately smitten with her, he fell in love and Olivier became his mistress. Suddenly, Picasso no longer dwelled in a state of mourning, and his artistic technique would reflect his transition away from sadness.

The works Picasso painted from the latter half of 1904 through 1906 are referred to as comprising his Rose Period. The descriptor takes its name from the fact that Picasso favored a palette filled with gradations of rose-colored tones. The iconography of the rose also evokes romance, reflecting Picasso's relationship with Olivier, who was his first serious love interest. It is not difficult to see how the freewheeling sensibility of Olivier cohered with that of Picasso. Although Picasso was just 23 years of age, he had already shifted locations numerous times and no doubt appreciated the equally bohemian nature of his new lover. Indeed, her life story was perhaps more adventurous than that of Picasso. Born Amelie Lang, Olivier ran away from home at 19 years old, and by the time she met Picasso in Paris, she had already been married and divorced, the victim of an abusive relationship. The same age as Picasso, Olivier and Picasso held a shared distaste for bourgeois mores and lived together for several years.

As the title would suggest, the main shift in painting style for Picasso during the Rose Period involved color. The blue tones of the Blue Period gave way to gradations of red color, the subjects of the paintings were less explicitly realistic, and the compositions were generally less naturalistic. A characteristic example of Picasso's style from 1904-1906 can be seen in his *Nude with Joined Hands*, completed in 1906.

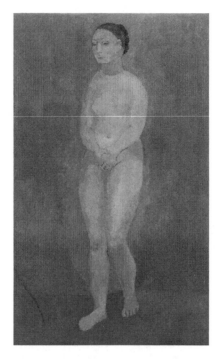

The painting continues the expressive use of color Picasso had inaugurated during the preceding Period of his career, as the background contains gradations of red and pink tones. The nude figure in the painting is Olivier herself, and she stands with an almost indistinct sunset in the background. Although the painting ostensibly portrays a scene in nature, Picasso reduces the natural surroundings to the interplay of pink and red hues, and the ambiguous setting makes it such that the scene has little of the documentary quality of the Blue Period. With Olivier as his muse, Picasso began painting more and more portraits, completing roughly 60 of Olivier alone.

While it is true that the Rose Period corresponded with a period of renewed vigor for Picasso, it is also the case that there are misunderstandings concerning the works completed from 1904-1906. The canonical reception of the Rose Period is that it exists in a binary with the preceding Blue Period, with the paintings from 1901-1904 reflecting deep anguish and those from 1904-1906 exuding celebratory joy. However, even a cursory glance at the paintings Picasso completed during the Rose Period reveals little of the joy that has been labeled as characteristic of the time period. Indeed, the nude in the painting (Olivier) fails to meet the gaze of the viewer, not unlike the subjects of the paintings from the Blue Period. Her joined hands suggest embarrassment at being looked at, and her facial expression is somber. Although her body is not gaunt in the manner of the subjects painted in the Blue Period, there is little sense of the *joie de vivre* one would expect from the period's title.

Even if the Rose Period represented less of a departure from the Blue Period than one might expect, the period nevertheless held importance in Picasso's development as an artist. In particular, while living in Paris he became heavily influenced by the Fauvist movement, highlighted by the paintings of Henri Matisse. The Fauves (which translates to "Wild Beasts") were a group of artists, including Matisse, Andre Derain, and Louis Valtat, who utilized bright, vibrant colors and quick, loose brushstrokes. Instead of conveying reality, the Fauves sought to distort and fragment it through utilizing eclectic color combinations and juxtaposing shapes. While Picasso's works from the Rose Period do not have the boldness one finds from the Fauvist style, it is nevertheless the case that the bright hues of the Rose Period borrowed heavily from the Fauvist style. In a sense, works such as *Nude with Joined Hands* represent the conflation of the somber mood of the Blue Period with the vibrant aesthetic of the Fauvist style.

Although the Rose Period is most famous for the rose-colored portraits Picasso completed during the period, Picasso also painted other subjects during this time, including circus performers. One of the most famous examples of such a work is *Family of Saltimbanques* (1905), which portrays a family of traveling circus performers. The theme of the circus was one that Picasso would revisit many times over his career, including a period in which he worked for a ballet troupe, and Picasso had a strong regard for the circus subjects. While living in Paris, Picasso frequented the Medrano Circus in Montmarte, which may have supplied his inspiration for the subject matter. Additionally, the circus performers can be interpreted as a reference to Picasso's own gypsy ancestry.

Although it is classified as one of the foremost works completed during the Rose Period, *Family of Saltimbanques* exhibits traits associated with the Blue Period. For example, the characters do not face each other, like the subjects of Picasso's *La Vie*, and though they belong to the same circus troupe, they exist in isolation from one another, as though they inhabited separate spatial registers. None of them smile, nor do they meet the gaze of the viewer. The characters appear lost within the desolate landscape, and while the costumes would superficially suggest an air of gaiety, the painting is one of alienation. Ultimately, while the title "Rose Period" suggests it was the time in which Picasso's mood lightened, this impression is not substantiated by the actual paintings from the period.

Chapter 4: Early Cubism and African Influence

"How can you expect a beholder to experience my picture as I experienced it? A picture comes to me a long time beforehand; who knows how long a time beforehand, I sensed, saw, and painted it and yet the next day even I do not understand what I have done. How can anyone penetrate my dreams, my instincts, my desires, my thought, which have taken a long time to fashion themselves and come to the surface, above all to grasp what I put there, perhaps involuntary?" – Pablo Picasso

While the majority of 1904-1906 was spent in Paris, Picasso also conducted some traveling during this period. Most notably, in 1905 he traveled to Holland for three weeks with his friend Tom Schilperoort, and while there he met the famous writer Gertrude Stein and her brother, Leo Stein. The Steins were devoted art collectors with a preference for avant-garde art, and they held Picasso's work in high regard; in fact, they would be partly responsible for the flowering reputation Picasso enjoyed in the following years. Picasso would become good friends with the Steins, and later in 1905 he would travel with them for a brief trip to Gosol, Spin. While there, the Steins introduced him to Henri Matisse, who was already recognized as a major figure in the international art scene.

Picasso's portrait of Gertrude Stein, 1906

Absorbing the influence of artists such as Matisse and Paul Cezanne had a major impact, and it was not merely limited to the use of bold colors that Picasso had gleaned from the Fauvism movement. Indeed, where the works of Matisse and Cezanne lay the foundations for cubism through their fragmented compositions, Picasso would make the cubist aesthetic even more pronounced. One of the earliest examples of Picasso's cubist technique is *Portrait of Gertrude Stein* (1906). Although the painting has little of the vibrant color that characterized the works from the Rose Period, *Portrait of Gertrude Stein* is far more experimental. Throughout the composition, the shapes are jagged and do not combine to form a coherent sense of space. Moreover, this impression relates to Stein's body itself; the traditional objective for portraiture is to achieve as close a likeness as possible to the subject, and it is clear that Picasso had far different objectives. Rather than attempting to portray her outward appearance, he instead focused on capturing a sense of existential malaise, which is achieved through the body's estrangement from its surroundings and the vacancy of Stein's facial expression.

The ghastly vacancy of Stein's facial expression also reflects the influence of African masks, which had strongly influenced Picasso during the time period. He was fascinated by the materiality of the faces and their threatening nature. One can see the influence of the African mask in Stein's face, as the pale white face and ovular eyes exude the exotic primitivism of African Art. After viewing the portrait, Stein famously commented that it did not resemble her, as she was just 32 at the time and Picasso made her appear far older, to which Picasso replied that eventually Gertrude would resemble her portrait. In the end, Picasso focused more on conveying the psychology of the individual more than reproducing their physical appearance.

The most famous example of the influence of African Art on Picasso was his famous *Les Demoiselles d'Avignon*, completed in 1907. In the painting, Picasso portrays a quintet of prostitutes, and though the title references Avignon, France, the inspiration for them also came from Picasso's past ventures into the red-light district of Barcelona. One of the most noticeable departures from Picasso's past works is that three of the women directly address the viewer, engendering a confrontational dynamic. The threatening quality of the women's faces borrows from a lineage of symbolist art, made most famous by Gustave Moreau, involving the castrating female. Moreau's paintings, such as *The Apparition* (1876), convey the woman as a threatening figure who tempts men through her sexuality but can only cause harm. The reasons for the subject matter of *Les Demoiselles d'Avignon* are varied; Picasso's relationship with Fernande Olivier had soured, and he held a slight misogyny toward the female gender that was complicated by his erotic fixation with them.

While the theme of the castrating female is certainly relevant to any consideration of Picasso's career, the most notable aspect of the painting is the wealth of citations to other paintings and mediums. One of the dominant themes of the painting is the way in which it synthesizes artistic techniques and mediums, as though Picasso wanted to combine all of the art he loved into one composition. The most obvious reference involves African masks, a motif that is especially pronounced with the two figures on the right. The face of the woman on the upper right also resembles that of a wild animal, which may constitute a reference to the Fauvist movement. Hilton Kramer and others have argued that the painting is a response to Matisse's *Joy of Life* (1906). While this is certainly possible, a more obvious reference is to Cezanne's *The Bathers* (1898-1905), which also featured a cluster of women painted in an abstract, jagged manner. However, the comparison between Matisse and Picasso cannot be ignored; both men focused on the nude female, but while Matisse celebrated them, Picasso viewed women with distrust. As Milton Viederman notes, Picasso's motif of the castrating female can be attributed to his "morbid concern about bodily deterioration and fear of death," while Matisse saw women as worthy of "affection and approbation".

Another medium referenced in the painting is sculpture. By 1907, Picasso had become a prolific sculptor, and the woman on the far left of *Demoiselles* represents a likely reference to sculpture. The profile view, as well as the fact that her entire body is shown, suggest that Picasso wanted to incorporate sculptural motifs in the work. The faces of the three women to the left also reflect the large features associated with Iberian sculpture. By incorporating elements of painting, sculpture, and African mask, Picasso synthesizes artistic mediums from around the world.

Chapter 5: Analytic and Synthetic Cubism

"The artist is a receptacle for emotions derived from anywhere: from the sky, from the earth, from a piece of paper, from a passing figure, from a spider's web... This is why one must not make a distinction between things. For them there are no aristocratic quarterings. One must take things where one finds them." – Pablo Picasso

As 1907 progressed, Picasso became even more resolute in his rejection of representational art. During that year, he met Georges Braque, who would be his artistic brother over the next several years. The two developed analytic cubism, an artistic movement that sought to fragment real-life objects into small shapes that, taken together, formed a recognizable motif. Picasso's *Portrait of Ambroise Voillard* (1910) represents one of the most famous examples from this period. The subject's body is hardy distinguishable, as Picasso subordinates accurate representation in the interest of juxtaposing shapes. In the analytic cubist tradition, the shapes come together at the center of the composition and the viewer can distinguish the subject's face.

During his analytic cubism phase, Picasso split time between Paris and Barcelona, and he was exposed to other avant-garde artistic movements that flowered during the time period. Two particularly noteworthy developments were The Blue Rider movement (a subset of German Expressionism) and Italian Futurism. The Blue Rider was comprised of a faction of German artists, including Wassily Kandinsky, Franz Marc, Paul Klee, and August Macke, who shared a mystic sensibility and emphasized the supernatural powers of nature. Although Picasso had little intellectual similarity with the movement, their formal technique appealed to him and influenced his more mature cubist style. In particular, the use of bold, saturated colors and primitive, almost childlike shapes were attractive to Picasso.

Italian Futurism was another prominent contemporary artistic and political movement whose members included Filippo Tommaso Marinetti, Giacomo Balla, and Umberto Boccioni. More overtly political than either Picasso's own work or that of The Blue Rider, the Futurists emphasized the power of technology. Balla's *Abstract Speed + Sound* (1913-1914) exemplifies the Futurist style, exuding the sense of speed associated with technology. Moreover, the abstract composition bears resemblance to the analytic cubist style evinced through works such as

Portrait of Ambroise Voillard.

Abstract Speed + Sound

Picasso and Braque continued painting analytic cubist works until 1912, when they modified their style substantially and created what is referred to as "Synthetic Cubism." The impetus for Synthetic Cubism was the need to incorporate objects from everyday reality into the composition, thereby "synthesizing" real-life objects into a composition. Picasso's *Still Life with Compote Glass* (1914-1915) exemplifies the Synthetic Cubist approach. The composition includes many different textures, objects, and materials, combining to form a collage that appears improvised and highly arbitrary. The spontaneity of the composition is reinforced by the title, which is banal to the point that it sounds as though it was devised instantaneously.

An important aspect of *Still Life with Compote Glass* is the way in which the letters "JOURN" and "AL" appear in the center of the composition. Through incorporating the cover of a journal, Picasso incorporates artifacts culled from everyday life, a novel approach in that it ran counter to the belief that art should exist separate from the "real world." By incorporating "found" objects into his compositions, Picasso added a documentary realism that anticipated the use of "found" objects in the Dada movement following World War II.

In addition to painting, Picasso popularized cubist sculpture during the World War I years. Similar to his paintings, he focused on incorporating different materials and "found" objects. An example of such a sculpture is *Mandolin and Clarinet* (1912), in which the musical instruments are comprised through combining a number of different materials. In sculptures such as this one, Picasso also demonstrated a refined ability to shape wood into different shapes to comprise the shape of the object. During this period, as in Analytic Cubism, the use of titles was especially crucial in ensuring that the viewer grasped the subject matter.

Chapter 6: World War I, Marriage, and the Ballet

While Picasso was shifting from Analytic to Synthetic Cubism, he underwent significant changes in his personal life. After over six years with Fernande Olivier in an on-and-off relationship, Picasso finally separated from her permanently, an in 1913 his father died. Don Jose Ruiz was already over 40 years old at the time his son was born, and he was already 76 when he died, despite Pablo's relative youth. Consequently, while the death of his father filled Picasso with sadness, it was not as tragic as the death of his young sister 18 years earlier. Picasso also mourned the death of Eva Gouel, who had been Picasso's mistress during his relationship with Fernande Oliver.

With the arrival of World War I, Picasso traveled to Italy, where he worked as a stage designer for the Ballets Russes troupe, designing curtains, decorations, and wardrobes. He also cultivated friendships with various artistic luminaries, most notably poet and filmmaker Jean Cocteau, and during this period he was introduced to the opulent lifestyle of high society. The most significant production in which Picasso was involved was *Parade*, for which Picasso designed the backdrop, the largest painting he ever made.

Picasso remained with the Ballets Russes for several years, and it was while working for the company that he met his first wife, ballet dancer Olga Khoklava. She was 10 years younger than him and had been estranged from her family as a result of the Russian Revolution. Picasso met her while in Italy in 1917 and proposed to her in 1918.

Picasso's decision to marry was surprising since he had always eschewed married life and had steadfastly avoided marrying Fernande Olivier, Eva Gouel, and the other mistresses with whom he had maintained relations. However, by 1918 Picasso was already 37 years old, and as he progressed through middle age, he realized that he could no longer wait to start a family. Picasso was actually engaged to marry a separate mistress of his, Irene Lagut, but she went against her word and called off the engagement.

On the surface, Picasso and Olga made an unlikely pair, as she was shy and evasive while Picasso was outgoing and gregarious. Olga had low self-esteem, to the extent that the critic Charles Morice has suggested that she suffered from a mental health disability of some kind, and it is likely that she desired the domineering presence of Picasso. The marriage between Picasso and his wife was hardly romantic, although they did have a son, Paulo, in 1921. Despite starting a family, however, Picasso never embraced domestic life and continued to have affairs with other women.

After the conclusion of World War I, he, Olga, and Paulo moved back to Paris, but Picasso continued to work for the ballet company until 1925, and he even crafted the stage design for Igor Stravinsky's *Pucinella*. However, according to Picasso's biographer, John Richardson, by the early 1920s Picasso had grown irritated with the ballet.

Chapter 7: Surrealism and Politics

While living in Paris during the 1920s, Picasso produced some of the works for which he is most famous. In 1921, he completed *Three Musicians*, a late example of Synthetic Cubism.

The work retains the collage aesthetic of past paintings like *Still Life with Compote Glass*, but he returned to using human subjects. Picasso pieced together (with the paintbrush) objects of different color and width, arriving at a composition that corresponded with its title. Also of note is the costume donned by the musician in the middle, which recalls that of Picasso's *Harlequin* (1914), as well as the circus outfit worn by one of the subjects in *Family of Saltimbanques* (1905). However, unlike Picasso's early *Family of Saltimbanques*, the mood of this painting is more cheerful and almost silly. Through invoking elements of past works, Picasso exhibited a sense of self-referentiality that would grow even more pronounced in his later works.

Although it remains one of his most famous works, *Three Musicians* is somewhat anomalous among the works Picasso produced after the conclusion of World War I. In general, he shifted toward painting more recognizable subjects, particularly mothers and daughters, and the period is often referred to as his Classical Period. A representative example from the period is *Mother and Child* (1921).

Unlike the figures from the cubist periods, the subjects are easily identifiable. Moreover, their rounded and almost flabby features constitute a clear departure from the emaciated subjects Picasso painted during his Blue Period, or even those of the Rose Period. The faint smile on the baby's face suggests that he is playing with his mother, and the mother appears to approve of his behavior.

As with any painting portraying a mother and child, this work can be compared with the Madonna and Child symbol that is so popular with Renaissance and Byzantine art. The palette is more monochromatic than that of *Three Musicians*, and the bodies have a timeless, prehistoric quality. It is immediately apparent that the mood of *Mother and Child* is more playful and cheery than traditional Madonna and Child compositions. Despite all of the death that Picasso had been forced to face during his life, Picasso emphasized the joys of parenthood, and with this work, viewers can sense that Picasso wanted to celebrate life through art, a descriptor that is commonly associated with Picasso to this day.

Despite his turn toward producing more cheerful artwork, Picasso's marriage was not a successful one. He exhibited little interest in raising his child, and he had countless mistresses.

Even so, he did not separate from Olga until 1925, and since he was reluctant to lose a significant amount of his fortune, Picasso refused to divorce her. They would remain married until her death in 1955.

The 1920s were significant in Picasso's career, as the decade marked his turn toward Surrealism. Picasso met Surrealist painters Joan Miro and Salvador Dali, and he would begin attending Surrealist meetings in the middle of the decade. The Surrealists were similar to Picasso in that they were invested in portraying psychological reality, but they were concerned with representing the unconscious, whereas Picasso had always been more focused on conveying conscious thoughts. The Surrealists were also more interested in creating a tactile sensation through their works. While Picasso could never be considered a true Surrealist, he shared a similar focus on abstraction and painting non-naturalistic compositions.

As the 1920s progressed, Picasso did manage to cultivate at least one meaningful romantic relationship with Marie-Therese Walter, and like many of Picasso's mistresses, Walter would serve as his model for a time. In 1935, he had a daughter with her named Maya, and by then he had already been named director of the Prado Museum in Madrid. He focused on sculpture and refined his Surrealist technique, having established a sculpture studio at the Boisgeloup Castle in Normandy in 1931. However, Picasso constantly remained on the move, and he continued to split time between France and Barcelona.

The early 1930s also saw Picasso produce some of his most famous works. He largely abandoned the Classicist works of the 1920s, instead returning to the abstraction of his Synthetic Cubist paintings. An example of the abstract works of the early 1930s is *Nude and Still Life* (1932).

Without the title, there is no way of knowing the subject matter. In a sense, Picasso technique is highly democratic, as the viewer is afforded the liberty to piece together the composition however they like. Picasso's use of the curved line is also prominent in this work and other ones of the period. While paintings like *Mother and Child* (1921) featured rounded shapes, the effect is even more pronounced in *Nude and Still Life*.

Another topic for consideration when it comes to Picasso's early 1930s paintings is the influence of Matisse. In particular, the use of the oval shape was a signature of Matisse, who was revered for his ability to draw lines, and the domestic shape also recalls Matisse. In the 1920s, an exhibition featuring Picasso and Matisse was in large part responsible for Picasso's rise to fame, and he always acknowledged Matisse as an influence. To this end, it is not unreasonable to infer that Picasso's more lighthearted works, particularly those produced in the early 1930s, reflect some degree of homage to Matisse.

Matisse

As the 1930s progressed and political turmoil surfaced, Picasso became more politically active than ever before. Despite associating with avant-garde artists for much of his adult life, Picasso had never taken a strong political stand, but that changed as the Spanish Civil War began. Picasso was adamant in his support for the Republicans, and even though he moved to Paris during this period, he was vociferous in his advocacy for the Spanish Republic. In the wake of the Guernica bombing, in which the entire town was bombed by German and Italian airplanes fighting for the Nationalists, Picasso was commissioned to paint the work that is recognized as perhaps his most famous.

Named after the town that was bombed, *Guernica* (1937) was painted relatively quickly, even by Picasso's accelerated standards, and he completed it in just under three weeks. Enormous in size, *Guernica* stands as a giant mural, measuring 11.5 feet tall and 25.6 feet wide. The painting contains a wealth of metaphors. For example, the bull and horse represent Spanish culture, the light bulb can be seen as a metaphor for the sun, and the clenched fist represents the Communist symbol for group solidarity.

Formally, Guernica represents a significant departure from the cheerful works completed during the early part of the decade. The palette is replete with white, black, and gray tones, and the absence of color is a metaphor for the horror of war. Additionally, the newspaper references the means through which Picasso learned of the atrocity. The painting's large size is also crucially important. Historically, large-scale paintings and murals were reserved for works of religious significance, and by painting the destruction of war on such a large scale, Picasso elevates the atrocity of war to the importance of religious painting. In this regard, the painting is similar to Francisco Goya's *The Shootings of May Third 1808* (1814), which deployed large scale painting to similar effect.

The exhibition history surrounding *Guernica* is also of great significance. The painting was first shown at the Paris International Exposition during the 1937 World's Fair in Paris. Subsequently, Picasso refused to allow it to be shown in Spain until after the reign of Nationalist leader Francisco Franco had ended. Following the Paris exhibit, the painting went on a world tour and was then shown in the United States, mainly at New York City's Metropolitan Museum of Art, for over a decade. Only after Franco's death was the painting approved for exhibition in Spain, and in 1981 it was shown for the first time in Spain at the Prado Museum in Madrid.

Chapter 8: A More Cheerful Style

The late 1930s were difficult for Picasso not only because of the Spanish Civil War but also because of the death of his mother in 1938, as well as the subsequent beginning of World War II. By this point, Picasso had also separated from Marie-Therese Walter, and he began a relationship with Dora Maar.

In 1939, Picasso moved to Royan, France with his friend Jaime Sabartes and Dora Maar, and he remained productive throughout the rest of the decade. As with previous lovers, Picasso treated Maar as a muse and completed numerous portraits of her, including *Portrait of Dora Maar* (1937).

In *Portrait of Dora Maar* (1937), the subject is considerably more legible than his paintings from earlier in the decade, even as there remains a fragmented quality. The left half of Dora's body faces a separate direction from the right, as though her right side existed at a separate moment in time, and as though she had turned to look behind her. The impression of motion being conveyed recalls earlier avant-garde compositions such as *Nude Descending a Staircase* (1912) by Marcel Duchamp, as well as the works of the Italian Futurists. However, Picasso's palette contains bright, cheerful colors, and the subject wears a smile, reflecting a lighthearted mood reminiscent of Matisse.

At the end of the 1930s, Picasso continued to deploy motifs associated with past works, a tendency exhibited in *Night Fishing at Antibes* (1939). Indeed, the grand scale and abstract, chaotic composition bear resemblance to *Guernica*, while the use of bright color is less bleak and suggests that Picasso had come to terms with the destruction of the Spanish Civil War.

During World War II, Picasso elected to remain in Paris, despite the fact that he allegedly contained Jewish ancestry. While his art was considered "degenerate" by the Nazi party, he had connections through Arno Breker (a favorite sculptor of Adolf Hitler) and Andre-Louis Dubois, who had influential sway with the Vichy government running occupied France, and in May 1942, his friend Maurice Toeska renewed his residency papers. During the war, Picasso painted using smuggled materials, and his palate reflected his sadness for the conflict. He began writing more poetry, and in 1940 he completed a play, *Desire Caught by the Tail*.

As the 1940s progressed, Picasso's spirits were low; he had always abhorred death and grew tired of the continuous armed conflicts ravaging Europe. Making matters worse, a collection of degenerate art, including works by Picasso himself, was burned by the Germans. Finally, Picasso aligned himself with the French Popular Front, and in 1944 he embraced the Communist Party. Although he would never have the political fervor of some of his Communist cohorts, Picasso strongly supported what he saw as a strong anti-war sentiment from the party. His opposition to all forms of combat continued following the war; in preparation for the World Peace Conference of 1949, he completed a painting of a peace dove, and he was twice awarded the International Stalin Peace Prize. After the war, he created *Massacre in Korea* (1951), a painting that opposed the United States' involvement in the Korean conflict.

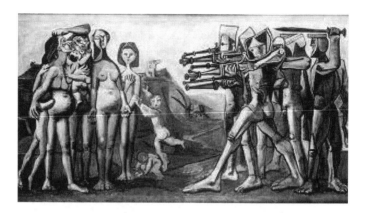

With *Massacre in Korea*, Picasso not only protested the United States' involvement overseas but also made reference to past works of his. The grouping of the family on the left recalls the wandering circus troupe from his early *Family of Saltimbanques*, and while his earlier work conveyed the alienation associated with the circus lifestyle, the later work adopted an even more despairing style and conveyed the brutality of war.

While Picasso's political involvement was not always cheerful, his personal life included some positive events, including his romantic relationship with Francoise Gilot, a woman 40 years younger than himself. With Gilot, he would have two more children: Claude (born in 1947) and Paloma (born in 1949). Despite that, he never married Gilot, and in fact he remained married to Olga until her death nearly a decade later.

Artistically, Picasso's life flourished throughout the 1940s. By now an international celebrity, Picasso's work acquired even greater acclaim with an exhibition at the Museum of Modern Art entitled "Fifty Years of His Art." Picasso also opened a studio with the famous lithographer Fernand Mourlot, where he refined his lithography technique. In 1947, he moved to Provence, where he would live for nearly a decade, and in 1953 he separated from Gilot and began a relationship with Jacqueline Roque.

Chapter 9: Final Years

By the mid-1950s, Picasso had reached old age, a subject for which he bore deep resentment. Always interested in young women, it frustrated Picasso to no end that his romantic appeal had begun to dwindle, but a major development in his personal life occurred in 1955 when his first wife died and he was again free to marry. At the time, he was already in a relationship with Jacqueline Roque, but the two would wait several years before marrying, finally becoming husband and wife in 1961, the same year Picasso turned 80.

In his old age, Picasso's art became retrospective and intensely physical. During this period, he completed many studies of the works of past artists, and he also painted literary subjects by reworking them with his characteristic loose brushstrokes. One of his better-known works from this period was *Don Quixote*, which portrays the eponymous character alongside his sidekick, Sancho Panza. The work has the primitive, sketchy quality of children's art, a trait with which Picasso was highly aware. Indeed, the late portion of his career reflects an obsessive quest to reacquire the artistic innocence of childhood, as evidenced by his quotation that "All children are artists. The problem is how to remain an artist once he grows up."

Picasso's late works also contained numerous revisions of the works of other artists, including Velazquez and Manet. In particular, Velazquez's *Las Meninas* (1656) was an object of fascination for Picasso, as he painted a total of 58 studies of the work. Velazquez's original work is famous for its use of different vantage points, but Picasso takes the theme even further, to the point that there is no clear subject. The objective is to confound the viewer, but at the same time the grin of the figure in the upper left establishes a playful tone.

Picasso's final paintings also included many compositions of young women, the majority of which were deeply erotic in nature, and during this period, he also completed an increasing number of engravings. Regardless of medium, Picasso made art continuously, and for him the flow of life was inextricably associated with artistic creation. In 1970, he donated over 900 works to the Picasso Museum in Barcelona, and many of the works continue to reside there today.

Continuing to work from the south of France, Picasso and Jacqueline Roque enjoyed entertaining guests, and Picasso was a lively entertainer who enjoyed his wine and spirits as well. Finally, on April 8, 1973 Picasso died while entertaining guests at his castle in Provence. His last words were reputed to be, "Drink to me, drink to my health, you know I can't drink any more."

Chapter 10: Picasso's Legacy

"A friend built a modern house and he suggested that Picasso too should have one built. But, said Picasso, of course not, I want an old house. Imagine, he said, if Michelangelo would have been pleased if someone had given him a fine piece of Renaissance furniture, not at all." - Gertrude Stein

In *Theory of the Avant-Garde*, Peter Burger categorizes two distinct variations of avant-garde artists, and the distinctions constitute a useful introduction through which to understand Picasso:

"Two philosophical and historical modes of understanding the avant-garde can be distinguished. These modes have contrary anthropological, social, and philosophical implications. One proceeds from what seems to be an infinitely variable opposition between solidification and dissolution, representation and life, metaphysical closure and deconstruction, general and particular, quantity and quality. The other proceeds from the historical observation that the mass media and official, ideological discourses tend to destroy and expropriate individual "languages" in the interests of domination." (xv-xvi).

The latter classification refers to avant-garde artists who are concerned with the industry of art, making overtly political works that critique the ideology of the industry. While it is true that all art is political, whether or not it chooses to exist as such, the second definition does not cohere with Picasso's sensibility or his artwork. Rather, Picasso was an avant-garde artist in the tradition of Burger's first definition, an artist who was obsessed with the act of making art and constantly explored tensions surrounding the oppositions between "solidification and dissolution, representation and life, metaphysical closure and destruction, general and particular, quantity and quality." This analysis of Picasso's life and career accounts for the constant experimentation that both defined him as an avant-garde artist and made his career so vast and difficult to assess.

Picasso's career is intimidating in its breadth, which is somewhat ironic given that his personality was genial and pacifist. In the years following his death, his reputation has not suffered, and he remains perhaps the most famous artist of all time. He refined Cubism more than any other artist, and as Jeoraldean McClain notes, arguably his greatest signature involved his ability to destabilize the association between space and time that had always existed in art. Along these lines, Picasso has also been likened to Albert Einstein for his ability to disrupt traditional spatial relations. While it should be noted that the disrupting of space and time for which Picasso is famous was actually inaugurated by Post-Impressionist artists like Cezanne, Picasso was nevertheless the figure who popularized the theme more than any other.

In many ways, Picasso was the consummate romantic artist, a figure that could not live without women, wine, and art. His art was born out of the Romantic school, with a predilection for the grotesque, even as it also borrowed from the dark, Spanish Realist tradition initiated by Goya and Velazquez, and the figures from his Blue and Rose Periods owe much to El Greco. Two of Picasso's most prevalent topics were human suffering and sensual pleasure, and one of the most compelling tensions within Picasso's oeuvre is the balance between the two. Ultimately, Picasso was a *suis generis* talent who embodied the innovative Modernist spirit perhaps more than any other artist.

Bibliography

Burger, Peter. *Theory of the Avant-Garde*. St. Paul: University of Minnesota Press, 1984.

Connelly, Frances S. "Introduction." *Modern Art and the Grotesque*. Cambridge: Cambridge University Press, 2003.

Kramer, Hilton. "The Triumph of Modernism: The Art World, 1985-2005." *Reflections on Matisse*, 2006.

Ludwig, Hans, Jaffe, Chris, *Pablo Picasso*. Norwalk: Easton Press, 1983.

McClain, Jeoraldean. "Time in the Visual Arts: Lessing and Modern Criticism." *The Journal of Aesthetics and Art Criticism* 44.1 (1985): 41-58.

Miller, Arthur J. *Einstein, Picasso: Space, Time, and the Beauty that Causes Havoc*. New York: Basic Books, 2002.

Morice, Charles. *Le Christ de Carriere*. Paris: Edition de la Libre Esthetique, 1899.

Nadel, Ira. *Modernism's Second Act: A Cultural Narrative*. New York: Palgrave MacMillan, 2013.

"Pablo Picasso." Olga's Gallery. *Abcgallery.com*, n.d.

Penrose, Roland. *Picasso: His Life and Work*. Berkeley: University of California Press, 1981.

"Pablo Picasso and his paintings." *Pablopicasso.org*. 2009-Present.

Viederman, Milton. "An Unusual Relationship: The Final Encounter of Picasso and Matisse." *The Psychoanalytic Quarterly* 62 (1993): 615-627.